DON'T THROW THAT OUT

A Pennywise Parent's to Creative Uses for Over 200 Household Items

by

VICKI LANSKY

Illustrations by
Martha Campbell

March 20, 1999

Distributed to the book trade
Publishers Group West
Emeryville CA

The Book Peddlers
Deephaven MN

D1551107

Special editorial thanks to:
Suzanne Pohle, Julie Surma Davis, Carol Lowry, Robyn Martin, Bruce Resnick, Kathryn Ring, and Carla Simmons

The Book Peddlers
18326 Minnetonka Blvd
Deephaven MN 55391
(612) 475-3527

Publisher's Cataloging in Publication
(Prepared by Quality Books Inc.)

Lansky, Vicki.
     Don't throw that out! : a pennywise parent's guide to creative
uses for over 200 household items / by Vicki Lansky ; illustrations
by Martha Campbell.
     p. cm.
     Includes index,
     ISBN 0-916773-40-X

     1. Home economics. 2. Parenting. I. Title.

TX158.L35 1994   640
                                                      QB193-22377

PRINTED IN THE UNITED STATES OF AMERICA
94 95 96 97 98 99 12 11 10 9 8 7 6 5 4 3 2 1

introduction

Dear Mom, Dad or Caregiver,

This book is a favorite collection of mine. I've always loved having "other" uses for household items. I think the first time was when I learned that you can use peanut butter to get gum out of children's hair when I wrote *FEED ME I'M YOURS*. I've been addicted to collecting these ideas ever since.

Here is my collection of ideas specific to the needs of parents and caregivers. They're the things I've read about, heard from friends or have learned in writing my parenting books as well as those I've received in the mail for my *FAMILY CIRCLE* column. It is the logical follow-up to my book, *ANOTHER USE FOR...101 COMMON HOUSEHOLD ITEMS*. These are the special "little" ideas that can really mean A LOT to those of us with kids at home. I've put these pennywise ideas together in one easy-to-use, alphabetically organized book.

I wish I could say I've done them all (I haven't), but they have worked for someone—which is how I came to hear about them. So use your judgement when selecting those for your family since I can't guarantee each one. I know you'll find lots of gems here—just as I have.

Vicki Lansky

Other books by Vicki Lansky

- Feed Me I'm Yours
  - The Taming of the CANDY Monster
  - Practical Parenting Tips Yrs 1–5
    - Toilet Training
      - KoKo Bear's New Potty
        - Birthday Parties:Yrs 1-8
        - Welcoming Your
          Second Baby
          - A New Baby at
            KoKo Bear's House
            - KoKo Bear's
              Big Earache
            - Getting Your
              Child to Sleep...
              and Back to Sleep
          - Trouble-Free Travel
            with Children

- Baby Proofing Basics • Dear Babysitter Handbook
- Divorce Book for Parents • 101 Ways to Tell Your
Child *I Love You* • 101 Ways to Make Your Child Feel
Special • 101 Ways to Say *I Love You* (*for adults*)
- 101 Ways to be a Special Dad • Kids Cooking
- Microwave Cooking for Kids • Games Babies Play
- ANOTHER USE FOR...101 Common Household Items

To order any of the above, or to receive a *free* catalog of all books,
call 1-800-255-3379, or write to:
Practical Parenting, Dept DTTO, Deephaven, MN 55391

Table of Contents

ADULT USES FOR CHILDREN'S ITEMS

TOPIC INDEX

Your A to Z Pennywise Parent's Guide to Creative Uses for over 200 Common Household Items!

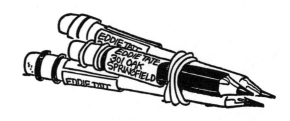

Address Labels
- Tape address labels to your child's school pencils for added insurance against loss.

- Add your address labels to the treats you give out at Halloween. Other parents will appreciate the identification. This is an especially thoughtful measure to take if your treats are homemade.

Airplane Discomfort Bags
- Save the bags from airline seat pockets. They come in handy for upchucks in other places—car travel, for example.

- Tuck a disposable diaper and a few prepackaged wipes into a bag to store in your glove compartment for that one time you're out of supplies or are unprepared.

1

Alcohol (rubbing)
- A few drops of rubbing alcohol in your child's ear canal after swimming can help to prevent "swimmer's ear."

Aluminum Foil
- Use aluminum foil to protect a bedwetter's mattress. Lay a towel over the foil.

- When applying an iron-on patch, place a piece of aluminum foil under the garment's hole so the patch won't stick to the ironing board cover.

- Polish the chrome on strollers, high chairs and playpens with a piece of wadded up foil. This works especially well on older items that have begun to look dull.

Answering Machine
- If you and your newborn need to sleep, turn on your answering machine and take a nap, unplugging the phone near your bed. Leave a message on the machine announcing your baby's name, weight, and wonderfulness.

Antacid
- Apply liquid antacid to the diarrhea diaper rash area during a diaper change. The antacid will offset the acid due to the continued exposure of diarrhea.

Applesauce

- Help an older child swallow a small pill by submerging it in a spoonful of applesauce.

Aquarium

- Use a softly lit fish tank as a "night light" in a child's room.

Audio Tapes

- Record the sounds of your crying baby and play the tape back to help induce sleep. It works! Many parents successfully record the sound of running water, a washing machine or a vacuum. Record it on an endless loop tape, and you can run it until you choose to turn it off.

- Tape your own recording of your child's favorite book for your child to use when you can't be there. The sound of your voice will add comfort and security. If it's for bedtime use, end it with *"Good night, I love you."*

- Tape record "letters" from your children to grandparents. This is nice when you can't be there for special occasions.

Baby Food Jars
- Use clean, dry baby food jars as take-along containers for cereals and other small treats.

- Make an emergency drinking cup out of a baby food jar. Clean and refill the jar. Punch a small hole down in the top of the lid and let baby drink away.

- Put prepared gelatin in an empty baby food jar and refrigerate to set. It's the perfect size dessert.

Baby Food Jar Lids
- Jar lids with the *"safety button"* feature can be used as a click toy.

- Use baby food jar lids to make large-scale checker sets for kids. Spray paint them black and red and make a board out of construction paper. No need to worry about lost checkers—these are easy to replace.

Baby Oil

- Cope with cradle cap (scale) by massaging oil into your baby's scalp. Loosen scales gently with a baby comb, then shampoo out. *(Don't continue if there is an infection. If the problem persists, see your pediatrician.)*

- Rub baby oil into plastic pants after washing to keep them from becoming dry and brittle. Or add baby oil to the rinse water when washing.

- Rub baby oil around the top and edges of a bandage to make removal easier.

Baby Powder

- Blow baby powder around the edges of a cast with a hair dryer to relieve itching.

- Clean up hot, sweaty, sand-covered kids with baby powder. Sprinkle it on their skin to soak up moisture, and the sand will fall off almost by itself.

Baby Wipes

- Clean baby's leather shoes with baby wipes.

- Use baby wipes in the car to clean up spills.

- Remove stains from chocolate to grape juice, on clothing and upholstery, with baby wipes.

- Use baby wipes to clean scrapes and cuts. Also soothes sunburn.

- Let a child "in training" use a baby wipe instead of toilet paper. It may be easier and seem more fun.

- Huggies brand baby wipes can be laundered and reused. Just wash as you would a cloth diaper. Laundered used wipes are also good as dust and cleaning cloths.

Baby Wipe Containers
- Store items such as audio tapes, photos, pencils, crayons and game pieces in baby wipe containers. Label and stack on shelves.

- Cut a slot in a baby wipe container lid to make a bank. Or cut several shapes and make your own homemade mini shape sorter for your child. Find items around your house that your child can put into the holes. Use care when selecting those items. Make sure they are not too sharp or too small.

Bags (plastic)
- Make a Hawaiian "grass" skirt by cutting narrow strips up the side of a large, green plastic lawn bag. Tape to fit.

- Cut the bottom off a plastic shopping bag with handles and slit it up the back. Use the handles as arm holes to turn the bag into a disposable bib for meal times or during arts and crafts activities. *(Don't leave a small child unsupervised with any form of plastic bag.)*

- Line the bottom of a travel potty with a small plastic garbage bag, and place a disposable diaper in the bottom to prevent sloshing. Dispose when convenient.

- Need to waterproof a mattress? If no rubber sheet is available, simply split a large garbage bag and place it under the sheet.

Bags (paper)
- Let kids blow up paper bags and smash them. Powerful fun!

- Make masks out of paper bags by cutting eyeholes and letting the kids draw faces on them.

- Use paper bags to make big building blocks for forts and castles. Lay the bag flat, fold the top over and crease. Fill with scrunched up newspapers. Fold the bag on the crease line and securely tape or staple it closed. Stack away!

Bags (mesh)

- Store bath toys in an old mesh bag from onions or oranges, or a garbage bag with holes for drainage. Hang it from the shower or faucet so excess water can drain right into the tub.

- Take a mesh bag to the beach. When it's time to leave, bag all the toys and dunk them in the water to remove sand.

- Make a basketball hoop out of a mesh bag. Cut the end off the bottom of the bag and thread a straightened metal coat hanger through the top, forming a circle. Hook the end over the top of the door.

Bags (self-closing)

- Use self-closing bags to make your toddler a board book. Overcast or machine stitch several small bags together along the bottom edge opposite the closing. Cut cardboard to fit inside each bag and slip magazine pictures or family photos on both sides of the cardboard. Change the pictures as often as you like.

- Store a damp washcloth in a self-closing bag and carry it in your purse or glove compartment for clean up. Sprinkle in a bit of baking soda to keep the cloth smelling sweet.

- Turn one into a pencil holder for use in your child's notebook by punching holes opposite the self-closing side. Freezer bags are stronger than regular sandwich bags. You may also want to reinforce the punched edge with duct tape.

- Carry a self-closing bag in your purse to collect all of those gum and candy wrappers that you collect from the kids. When the bag is full, empty it.

- Use larger self-closing bags for storing puzzle pieces and game items. The clear plastic makes it easy to see what is inside.

Baking Soda (for relief)

- To fight diaper rash, sprinkle a little baking soda in warm water and clean baby's bottom area. The baking soda soothes and helps to heal by neutralizing any acid.

- Pour half a box of baking soda in the bathtub to help relieve the itching from chicken pox, bug bites and sunburn.

Baking Soda (for clean up)

- Return baby's white shoes to their original luster by polishing them with baking soda and a damp cloth.

- Freshen your children's dolls with a paste made from of liquid dish detergent and baking soda. The combination removes stains—including ink! Get into the tiny crevices by dipping a toothbrush in baking soda and scrubbing.

- When your baby upchucks on your shirt, sprinkle the spot with baking soda. Let it dry and brush it off. Odor is gone. You might carry a small container of baking soda in your purse for such emergencies.

- After a wet bed accident, blot wetness with a towel, next sprinkle baking soda over the damp area and let it dry, then vacuum.

- Get rid of spaghetti, catsup, or crayon stains on your plastic high chair tray by sprinkling the dampened tray with baking soda. Rub tray with a damp cloth, then rinse.

- To clean a stuffed animal or fabric toy that can't be washed, shake it in a bag filled with baking soda. This will absorb the dirt and grime. Shake or vacuum the excess baking soda off.

Baking Soda (for crafts projects)

- Mix a "Rubbery Play Dough"—chemical-free—by cooking 2 cups baking soda, 1 cup corn starch and 1½ cups water together. Stir over medium heat until thickened. Spread the mixture on a plate and cover with a damp cloth until it's cool enough to handle. Knead the dough a couple of minutes until smooth. Add food coloring if desired. Store in the refrigerator in an air-tight container. Your child's creations may take two or three days to air dry or they can be baked in the oven on a low setting until dry. Paint with poster or acrylic paints. Finish with a layer of shellac or acrylic varnish.

- To make "Invisible Ink," dissolve 1 tsp baking soda in 2 tsp water and use this as ink to write an invisible message on a piece of paper. When the ink is dry, hold the paper near a light bulb. The writing will turn brown and be visible.

- Make a "Bouncing Snowflake Bowl" by putting: 1 cup water, ¼ cup vinegar, and 1 tsp baking soda in a clear bowl—such as a fishbowl. Add buttons, plastic confetti or small dry pasta pieces and watch them dance!

- Make a "Magical Inflating Balloon." First, put 2 tsp baking soda into a soda bottle with a funnel. Clean the funnel and use it to pour ⅓ cup vinegar into a balloon. Stretch the neck of the balloon over the mouth of the bottle and pull it down ¾ inch. Hold the neck of the balloon around the neck of the bottle and lift to drain the vinegar into the bottle. The reaction between it and the baking soda will cause fizzing and produce carbon dioxide gas, which will blow up the balloon. *(Caution: Do this in the kitchen sink for easy clean up.)*

• Let kids play chemist by mixing baking soda and vinegar and watching it boil and fizz in different containers. If you want an interesting comparison, put ½ cup of hot vinegar in one cup and ½ cup of chilled vinegar in another. Drop a teaspoon of baking soda into each cup and watch the difference.

• Make a "volcano" erupt in your kids' sandbox. Set a juice glass filled with vinegar inside the sandbox mountain. Add one tablespoon of baking soda and watch what happens!

Balloons

• A freshly laundered baby bonnet will retain its shape while drying if placed over a blown-up balloon.

• Fill a few small balloons with water and keep them in the freezer for dripless cold compresses for bumps and bruises or imaginary injuries.

• For a unique birthday party invitation, blow up a balloon, and while holding the end closed, write the date, time and other party details onto the balloon with a waterproof marker. Deflate, and put it in an envelope to mail.

- Make your child a "cluster of grapes" costume by tying 20 or more purple and/or green balloons to safety pins and attaching them to his or her clothing. Use different colored balloons for a "jelly bean" costume.

Balloons (helium-filled)

- Attach a helium-filled balloon to your toddler's wrist when in a crowd to help you keep track of him or her more easily.

- When camping, tie several helium-filled balloons to your tent so your kids can locate your campsite. *(Metallic helium-filled balloons last longer than rubber balloons.)*

- To help your child locate your spot at the beach, tie colorful balloons to the beach umbrella.

- Use helium-filled balloons as place cards at a child's birthday party by tying them to the chairs and writing the guests' name with a marker.

Bandana Scarf
- Use a bandana as a drool bib. Just tie or clip around the child's neck.

Bathtub Appliques
- Sew pieces of self-sticking bathtub appliques to the bottoms of pajama sleeper feet to prevent falls on slippery floors.

- Stick bathtub appliques to the bottom of a kiddie pool to minimize slipping and falling.

- Apply pieces of bathtub appliques around the sides of children's plastic cups to keep them from slipping out of wet hands.

Beach Towels
- Make an attractive bedspread for a child's bed with a BIG beach towel.

- Pin a large towel around your neck like a bib. It will keep you dry when bathing your baby and will also serve as an instant towel wrap for your little one.

Belt
• Use an old belt to secure a child in a grocery cart or in a restaurant high chair that no longer has a strap. An elastic belt would be even better.

Berry Baskets
• Use plastic berry baskets in the dishwasher to hold bottle nipples and prevent them from falling into the bottom of the dishwasher and becoming lost.

• Turn a berry basket upside down to make a cage for tiny toy animals.

• Make great geometric stencils for kids by cutting apart the panels of a berry basket. Cut hearts, stars and other shapes. Kids can use these to rub over for a stencil project or can trace around with a pencil.

• Weave ribbons or yarn through the open areas of a berry basket. Use a pipe cleaner for a handle. Fill with cellophane grass or a handful of straw to make May baskets or carriers for Easter eggs.

Bottles (detergent squeeze)
• Clean detergent squeeze bottles and fill them with water for the kids to use for a friendly fight on a hot day. Make certain all of the soap is out so none gets into eyes!

- Refill an empty, handy-size bottle with children's shampoo from a giant economy jar to eliminate spillage and waste.

- Fill a squirt bottle with pancake batter and let kids squirt squiggles into deep-frying fat. Drain and dust with powdered sugar. *(An adult should supervise frying procedures.)*

Bottles (plastic, gallon)
- Cut off the top third of a milk jug, leaving the handle. Use it for a party penny toss. The kids can keep the pennies that go in the jug. Or personalize them and give one to each child as a favor tote to fill with prizes.

- Cut a hole in the side of an empty, clean bleach jug opposite the handle to make a carryall for a toddler's Legos pieces or crayons. Sand down any rough edges.

- Turn one into a bird feeder. An old chopstick can be inserted below the opening as a perch.

Bottles (roll-on)
- After cleaning, refill an empty roll-on deodorant bottle with baby oil and just roll it onto your baby's skin instead of getting it all over yours.

• Refill a deodorant bottle with tempera paint for your children's art projects. Fill another with water to wet stamps and stickers, or with water and a white glue mixture for craft projects.

Bottles (small)
• Decorate a small bottle to "preserve" tears. Run for it each time a child cries. The game will soon ease the pain—and, one hopes, limit the tears.

Bottles (two-liter plastic)
• Cut three slits on one side of a two-liter plastic bottle. Insert the garden hose into the bottle neck and tape it shut. Turn on the water for some great water play.

• Use empty two-liter bottles for bowling pins. Filling them with sand or water will help them to remain upright. Use a basket-ball as the bowling ball.

Bungi Cords
• Secure cabinet door knobs together with short bungi cords so a child can't get into unsafe items in a cupboard.

• Stretch a taut bungi cord flat against a wall between two hooks so a child need only "slip" something under it. It can hold items in place such as stuffed animals, tall toys or even certain clothing items.

Buttons

• Sew buttons onto the wrists of your children's gloves. The gloves can then be buttoned into the buttonholes of your children's coats when they take them off.

• Use buttons to make a bean bag. These make an interesting, clicking sound. Or substitute buttons as markers for any board game.

Calendars

• Use *(and save)* an extra calendar to record special moments, sayings, activities or progress—especially during that first year. Save one each year with your mementos.

• Hang spare calendars in your older children's rooms for them
(*or you*) to record the day's events. Makes a great keep-
sake.

• Let your child practice writing numbers next to dates in the
squares on an old calendar.

• Leave a special calendar message for your child on an
important day. Cut around three sides of that special day's
square, creating a flap that can be opened. Write your note
on plain paper that you paste on the back of the calendar
page.

Candle
• For an unusual painting, have your child draw a design on a
sheet of white paper with a white candle or crayon. Then
have the child cover the entire sheet with paint. When the
paint dries, the original "invisible" drawing shows through.

Car Drink Holder
• Attach a car drink holder to your child's bed or crib to relieve
the inevitable request for a drink of water at bedtime.

Cardboard Boxes
• Use a large cardboard box as a "garage" for your child's
wheeled vehicles or toy trucks. Remove one side and paint
lines for parking spaces on the bottom of the box.

• Use a wine bottle box, with the dividers left in, for storing dolls or action figures.

Cardboard Tubes

• Fill toilet tissue tubes with candy or tiny toys, wrap the tubes in colored tissue and tie the ends with ribbon or yarn. Easy, inexpensive party favors!

• Or turn short tubes into musical "shakers" by filling them with dried beans and taping the ends closed. Different size beans will make different sounds.

• Make a kazoo by punching a small hole an inch from one end and covering the other end with waxed paper that is held snuggly by a rubber band. Have the kids blow or hum into the open end.

• Cover short or long cardboard tubes with adhesive paper and glue Velcro pieces on the sides. Then let children use them for making free-form constructions. Long tubes can also be used to construct a tent frame to be covered with a sheet or light weight blanket for an instant indoor playhouse.

• Send kids' special papers to and from school rolled in long tubes from paper towel rolls. Or use paper towel tubes to save special projects the kids have made. Carefully roll up and place inside.

- Help small children reach the light switches independently. Cut a rectangular hole a few inches from the end of a long cardboard tube. The child can hook this over the switch and turn lights off or on by moving the tube up and down.

- Turn a long cardboard tube into a bat for an indoor baseball game. Use a balloon for the ball. This is safer and easier on the house when kids are playing indoor baseball.

Cat Litter
- Keep an inch or two of cat litter in the bottom of your diaper pail to absorb odors. Line the pail with a plastic bag to hold dirty diapers.

- Spread cat litter over vomit on floors to absorb moisture and odor. Sweep up and dispose of.

Cereal
- Float cereal pieces, like Cheerios, in the toilet bowl so your son can practice his "aim" while toilet training.

Chalk
- Let your kids draw with chalk on driveways or patios. They can create massive murals, and highways for trucks, or oceans and islands for pirates. Hose down for clean up.

Christmas Bells
- Hang large bells on a door to alert you when a toddler is coming or going. And tie small bells to a child's shoestrings for the same reason.

- Bells attached to the lower branches of your Christmas tree will let you know when a curious toddler or pet is near.

Clothespins (clip)
- Clip a dish towel behind a child's neck for a large bib.

- Clip mittens together when your child takes them off to keep them in pairs.

- Use clip clothespins to keep motel drapes shut tightly while traveling. This will prevent unwanted drafts and light from reaching your sleeping child.

- Attach clip clothespins to a closet wall with a hot glue gun to hold a variety of items from gloves to laundry bags. Glue them to a board or wall above your baby's changing table to hang clothes, etc. A coat of paint to match or contrast would be wonderful.

Coffee Filters

- Poke the stick of a frozen treat through the center of a coffee filter. The drips will fall inside the paper, not on your child.

- Use coffee filters as disposable holders for popcorn, tacos, hot dogs or ice cream cones.

- Fold a paper filter in half at least three times, then cut out small pieces from the edges. Open, and you have a decorative snowflake.

- Fill a coffee filter with treats— for Halloween, a birthday party, etc. Tie with a ribbon and decorate with stickers.

Colanders

- Place a colander over a pan to keep the grease from splattering when kids are helping with the cooking.

- Let an old colander serve as a bath, beach or sandbox toy.

Cooler

- A large cooler can double as a tub in which to bathe small children when camping.

Correction Fluid
- Cover scuff marks on children's white shoes with correction fluid.

- At holiday time, paint snowflakes with correction fluid on the insides of your windows or glass storm doors. Remove the decorations by scraping them with a plastic straight edge.

Cotton Balls
- Cotton balls and cotton strips from pill bottles make great fake hair for children's brown bag masks. Dip the pieces of cotton in glue and stick them on the bag for hair or a beard.

- Or apply them directly to a child's face, using corn syrup as an easy to clean up facial glue.

- Attach a few cotton balls to the rear of a pair of white tights to make a Peter Cottontail costume.

Crockpot
- Heat up wet towels in your crockpot the next time you need a supply of hot, moist compresses to treat an injury.

Dental Floss
- Sew buttons on coats and sweaters with dental floss. It is much stronger than regular thread. Floss can also be tinted to match the garment by touching up with colored markers.

- Repair a torn mesh playpen with dental floss which is strong and can easily be manipulated through the mesh openings.

- Restring children's necklaces on dental floss. Let the kids use it for stringing beads and macaroni.

Denture Tablet
- Remove scum from a glass baby bottle by dissolving one denture tablet in a bottle that you've filled with hot water. Allow to stand for several hours before rinsing out.

Diaper Pin
- Pin the tab of a zipper sleeper to the yoke of the pajama to keep your child from unzipping it during nap or nighttime. Be careful if your child has the dexterity to open the pin.

Dish Drainer
• Use a dish drainer as a holder for children's books or records. The silverware section can hold crayons and pencils or rulers.

Dishpans
• Arrange dishpans on open shelves to organize small toys or toys with many small parts. Dishpans are just the right size for a child to carry around.

• Or use one to hold books and other items when traveling by car.

Dog Tag
• Have a pet tag engraved with your child's name, address and phone number to tie onto shoe laces when you're shopping or camping.

"Do Not Disturb" Sign
• Avoid newborn nap interruptions (or your naps), by hanging this handy hotel room sign on the door.

Dustpans
• Let a toddler use a dustpan as a snow shovel.

• Scoop up small toys with a dustpan when you need a quick clean up.

Egg Cartons

• Cut the bottom half of an egg carton into thirds, paint it and attach a pipe cleaner as a handle for an easy-to-make, four-egg Easter basket. Decorate it as you like.

• Use egg cartons as drawer organizers for small children's socks or other items.

• Let an egg carton serve as an organizer for a pebble, bottle cap or shell collection.

• An old egg carton makes a good cash register when kids play store.

- Make a game for kids by removing the top of an egg carton and marking the insides of the cups with the numbers 1, 2, and 3. Each child takes a turn throwing the same number of pennies. High score wins. Also use cartons for teaching young children to sort things by numbered sections.

Egg Poacher
- Warm up small portions of different baby foods in an egg poacher.

- Parts from an egg poacher make good toys to use in the sandbox.

Emery Boards
- Rough up soles of new hard-soled shoes with an emery board, so they will be less slippery.

- An emery board will remove oily dirt from a pencil eraser for a fussy school age child.

Erasers
- Remove scuff marks from the floor or remove crayon marks from walls with an eraser.

- Use an eraser to remove certain scuffs from white shoes.

Fabric Softener Sheets
• Do your kids have smelly sneakers? Stuff a fabric softener sheet or two into each shoe at night.

• Stuff a doll or small pillow with used fabric softener sheets.

• Does your child have fly away, static-ridden hair? Rub a fabric softener sheet over his or her hair and it will stay in place.

Fan
• Run an oscillating fan near the crib. The humming sound has a mesmerizing effect, and often puts a baby right to sleep.

Film Canisters (35mm)
• Use black plastic film canisters to make eyes when building a snowman.

• Turn one into a pocket Cheerios holder for your child.

• A 35mm film canister makes a good place to put milk or lunch money for the school-aged child.

Flashlights

• Attract an insect to come out of a child's ear by shining a flashlight into the ear canal. Do this in a darkened room.

• Illuminate a carved pumpkin with a flashlight, instead of a candle, as a safety measure.

• Use a penlight to follow the words in a book while reading to your child. *(P.S. A small flashlight makes a great gift for a preschooler.)*

Foam Rubber

• Glue a small piece of foam rubber to the inside of a barrette to help keep fine hair from slipping.

Food Coloring

• Let kids paint marshmallows with food coloring. Also let them paint cookies, either before or after baking. Use a new paintbrush when painting food.

• Add food coloring to milk or pancake batter to mark special days—red for Valentine's Day, green for St. Patrick's Day, for example.

• Use food coloring to turn plain cereals multi-colored, or add to milk for fun. Add blue to raw eggs before scrambling, to make Dr. Seuss's famous "green eggs and ham."

• In the winter, let kids paint in the snow with plastic squeeze bottles filled with water and food coloring.

Funnel
• Add a funnel to a child's stock of bathtub or sandbox toys.

Garbage Can
• Store outdoor toys in a big, plastic garbage can.

Garden Hose
• Slit old sections of a hose lengthwise and cover swing set chains to help provide a steadier grip for kids.

• Cut two lengths of an old hose and slit to make a pair of ice skate blade covers.

Garlic Press
• Use a garlic press to mash egg yolks quickly for baby food.

• Use a garlic press to produce hair texture for playdough/clay creations.

Gelatin
• Combine one three-ounce package of fruit-flavored gelatin with a cup of cold water. Let a child drink it all at once when you need a "binder" for a run-of-the-mill case of the runs.

Gift Wrap Paper
• Use pretty gift wrap paper to line baby's dresser drawers.

Gloves (cotton)
• Wear cotton gloves when bathing a newborn in a plastic bathtub or sink. The gloves will give you a better grip than bare hands.

• Cut off fingers from old cotton gloves to create finger puppet mice for storytime or puppet shows.

Gloves (rubber)

• For a great ice pack for kids, fill a transparent glove with water, tie off and freeze.

• Let kids blow up thin surgical gloves like balloons and decorate them.

• Make heavy duty rubber bands by cutting horizontal strips from the fingers, palms and wrist parts of old rubber gloves.

Glue

• Apply white glue to skin where small splinters, such as those from a cactus plant, are embedded. Let dry, then peel off. Most prickers will come off with the dried glue.

• Make a homemade version of Silly Putty by combining 2 parts liquid white glue with 1 part of liquid starch. Mix well and store in airtight container. *(Beware! This mixture has the same nasty characteristics as commercial Silly Putty, so be careful with clothes and carpet.)*

• Equal parts glue and liquid starch are very similar to GAK.

Gum Ball Machine

• Turn the old gum ball machine into a dispenser for healthy treats like nuts, cereals, yogurt-covered raisins and the like.

 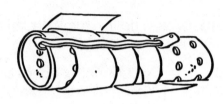

Hair Curlers

• Store hair ribbons neatly by wrapping them around a smooth hair roller. Secure them with a bobby pin.

• Slip a small hair curler on a bruised finger to protect it.

Hair Dryer

• Use the dryer--at a safe distance and on a low setting-- to dry a baby's bottom.

• Use a hair dryer on *high* to keep a hot compress hot.

• Speed dry wet boots, boot liners or shoes with a hair dryer — but not unattended.

• Crayon marks on washable wallpaper? Warm up the crayon wax with your hair dryer (on *high*) before wiping it away with a damp cloth.

• Make bandage removal easier by blowing hot air on the tape for a few seconds to soften the adhesive.

Hair Spray

• Spray hair ribbons lightly to keep them clean and stiff.

• Wipe up cut hairs from the child, the sink or the floor with a tissue dampened with hair spray.

• Remove most ballpoint pen marks from skin and clothing with a squirt of hair spray. Wipe off with a soft cloth.

• Make an inexpensive gift wrap by spraying the Sunday comics with hair spray. It seals the ink and gives the paper a nice gloss. Kids love it.

Hangers

• Bend a wire coat hanger into a circle, leaving the hook for a handle. Pour bubble solution into a wide, shallow baking pan, dip the hanger loop in and pull it gently through the air to make extra large bubbles.

• Straighten a wire hanger and use it as a marshmallow or hot dog holder for a camp fire roast. (*Don't use painted hangers!*)

Heating Pad
• Use a heating pad or a hot water bottle (*not too hot!*) to warm the crib before putting a new baby down.

Honey "Bear" Containers
• Wash out an empty honey bear container and fill with your child's favorite drink. Insert a straw through the top for a cute drink holder.

Hydrogen Peroxide
• Remove blood stains on white clothes by pouring hydrogen peroxide over the stained area. Let it bubble and then rinse.

"Ice Balls"
• Keep your child's milk or juice bottle cold and undiluted with frozen plastic "ice balls," that are sold for use in mixed drinks. Store in freezer.

Ice Cream
- Put one scoop of vanilla ice cream in a bowl of cold cereal instead of milk for a special afternoon treat.

Ice Cream Cones
- Fill a flat-bottom cone half-full of cake batter, bake and decorate, for individual special occasion cakes. In a microwave oven two cone "cakes" cook in about one minute.

- Serve lunch —tuna, cottage cheese, etc.— in a cone for a change of pace.

Ice Cream Pails
- Stash cleaning aids in closed buckets to keep them out of the reach of children.

- Create your own drop-in toy by cutting shapes into the lid of an old ice cream pail. Good choices might be a ball, a wooden block, or other pieces from your child's toychest.

Ice Cubes
- Place ice cubes in a baby sock, tie a knot in the end, and let a teething baby gnaw on it.

- Let your child suck on an ice cube after biting his or her tongue. Also a good way to deaden the taste buds before giving unpleasant tasting medicine.

- Use ice to numb the skin before removing a splinter.

- Place ice cubes in a sturdy plastic bag and hit with a hard object to make ice chips. These are good for older children to suck on after vomiting when liquids are restricted. Makes mouth taste fresher.

Ice Cube Trays
- Use a molded ice cube tray to hold socks, barrettes and hair clips, etc., in an organized fashion.

- Freeze pureed baby food in a molded ice cube tray and store the frozen food cubes in a freezer bag. Defrost or warm up food cubes as needed.

Inflated Swim Tube
- Put a child-sized swim ring around the waist of an infant who is just learning to sit alone. It will cushion tipovers.

Iron-On Patches
- Iron patches to the soles of footed pajamas to make them less slippery, or to the insides of the knee area on a pair of long pants or jeans.

Jewelry Box
- Donate your old jewelry box to your child. It may become a precious hiding place to hold treasures and secret collections.

Juice Cans (frozen)
- Good for a quick dripless ice pack on an injury.

Junk Mail
- Can be used for playing post office. Let your child have an old tote bag for the mail pouch.

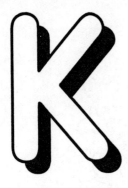

Key Ring
- Attach a key ring to children's zipper tabs on boots and/or jackets for easy zipping and unzipping.

Keys
- Old keys, with well-worn edges, can make a good, jingly baby toy. You know how much babies like to play with your keys, now give them a set of their own. Just tie clean keys securely onto a piece of ribbon, cord or use a spare key chain.

- Several old keys in a plastic container with a secure snap-on lid make an instant noisemaker for your toddler. Different size keys make different noises.

Kitchen Canisters
- Turn an old set of kitchen canisters into decorative holders next to your changing table to hold supplies.

Kneeling Pad
- When it comes time to start bathing your baby in a regular tub, a foam kneeling pad from your garden makes an excellent cushion between hard tile floors and your knees.

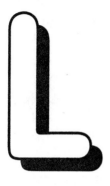

Ladder
- Lay an extension ladder across the end of the driveway to keep kids from riding bikes out into the street.

Laundry Baskets (plastic)
- Carry beach toys in a plastic laundry basket so you can easily rinse off the sand. Dunk it while filled with toys in the water and drain thoroughly before leaving the beach.

- Pad a rectangular plastic laundry basket for an instant infant bed for home or away from home.

- Use a round laundry basket in the bathtub to give support to a baby who sits up. Don't ever leave a baby unattended in the bath.

Lemons
- Let your kids write messages with a cotton swab using lemon juice as invisible ink. After the "ink" is dry, hold the paper near a hot light bulb (*not too close!*). The writing will turn brown and you'll be able to read the message.

• Whiten kids' discolored socks by boiling them for a few minutes in water with a few lemon slices or with lemon juice added.

Lemon-Shaped Plastic Containers

• Remove the inner plug from a lemon juice container with a fork tine, rinse it out well and fill it with water or juice. Replace the plug and screw top, and you'll have a unique, portable, personal drink container for your child.

• Fruit-shaped citrus dispensers are ready-made tree ornaments. Thread a 6-inch piece of yarn or ribbon through the little loop on the lid, tie the ends and hang. Let kids decorate them with glitter, paint, etc.

Life Saver Candies

• Lay these candies flat on the top of a frosted birthday cake to act as holders for birthday candles.

• Let kids string Life Savers on licorice whips or long ribbons to create fun necklaces to be taken home after a birthday party.

Lunch Boxes

• Carry snacks for kids in a lunch box while running errands. Having a special treat in their own container may soothe a hungry or tired child.

- Pack first aid supplies in an old lunch box. Keep in your car as a first aid kit.

Markers

- Draw a star, heart or I-love-U on an adhesive bandage with a marker to "speed heal" your child's injury.

Marshmallows

- Drop a large marshmallow into a flat-bottomed ice cream cone before adding ice cream, to minimize leaking. Use mini-marshmallows in pointed cones.

Muffin Tins

- Pour boiling water in muffin tins to warm up jars of baby food. Let sit for 5 minutes. Works well for bottles, too.

• Use a muffin tin to hold different colored paints for arts and crafts projects.

• Fill muffin tins for kid-size portions when making jello, pudding or other desserts.

Mug
• Use a plastic mug as a handled bowl for serving soup or cereal. It's easier for a child to manage.

Mug Racks
• Install a mug rack above the changing table to air dry plastic pants and hang other items.

• Put a mug rack in the hall closet to hold hats and mittens.

Nail Polish (clear)
• Cover decals on children's toys that will get a lot of wear with clear nail polish.

• To keep ends of satin or grosgrain ribbon from fraying, dab on a little clear polish. It seals the edges and will last through machine washings.

• Coat shoelace tips with clear nail polish if plastic ends are worn off.

• Use nail polish as an emergency glue on craft projects.

• Nail polish can also be used to repair leaks on inflatable toys. Deflate and give the hole several coats of this sealer.

Nail Polish (red)
• Highlight ounce marks on plastic baby bottles with a bright red polish.

• Paint a big red dot on the hot water faucet so a child will know which faucet is the hot one.

• Use nail polish to mark initials on the bottom of kids little cars or other small toys to identify them.

• For safety, paint the caps or lids of all containers holding poisons with red nail polish. Also paint a big "X" on both sides of these containers. Teach your child that anything with a red X-mark means "*Stop! DANGER!*"

Nail Polish Remover

• Use nail polish remover on a soft cloth to remove scuffs from patent leather or white vinyl shoes. Rub lightly.

• Use nail polish remover to get rid of ballpoint pen marks or paint from skin.

Napkin Holder

• Use a napkin holder as a stand for small books or records.

Necktie

• Turn dad's old tie into a snake toy or sea serpent by making a face at the large end and stuffing it with old nylons. Sew shut.

Netting (nylon)

• Secure a double layer of nylon netting around an electric fan to give added protection— but not a guarantee— against probing fingers.

Newspapers

• Use newspaper for the pattern paper to cut out your child's costume.

• Save newspaper comic sections for juvenile gift wrap or to use as a disposable tablecloth at a birthday party.

• Ask a child to describe the feelings of people pictured in the newspaper and why they might be feeling that way.

Nipples (from a baby bottle)

• Dispense liquid medicine to your baby by placing the correct dose in an open bottle nipple that you hold with your fingers.

• Use a bottle nipple in a penny bank that has lost it's plug.

Non-Stick Spray

• Oil squeaky hinges on a toy box, and wheels on a stroller or tricycle with a squirt of non-stick vegetable spray.

• Spray cookie cutters and other tools used to mold clay with a non-stick spray to keep clay from sticking.

• Before decorating windows with artificial snow, very lightly spray them with non-stick spray. It will make clean up easier when the holiday season is over.

Nylon Stockings

• Make your own inexpensive softball by stuffing an old sock with pantyhose and sewing the top closed. Stockings make good stuffing for dolls, pillows and toys.

• By securing a piece of a nylon stocking to a jar with a rubber band you can make a "breathable" insect home.

- Thread a coat hanger through the edge of a nylon stocking to make a pool skimmer to collect leaves and debris from your child's backyard pool.

- Use as a catch-all for collecting sea shells at the beach. The leg of the stocking will stretch quite a bit and be able to hold lots of shells. Water will drain through, too!

Olive Oil
- Use a few drops of olive oil when giving your baby a massage.

Oven Mitt
- Use thick oven mitts as sole replacements when pajama feet wear out. Cut to shape and sew in place.

Paintbrushes

- Store a big paintbrush in the car trunk and use it to remove sand from kids' feet before they get into the car.

- Also good for removing sand from buckets, shovels, and other beach stuff.

- Let a child "paint" the house with water and a clean paintbrush. The wetness will make the house look dark temporarily until the water dries.

- Clean a baby's bottle with a small, clean paintbrush if you don't have a bottle brush.

Paintbrush (sponge)
- Use a dampened sponge paintbrush to apply calamine lotion on a child coping with chicken pox or mosquito bites.

Paper Cups
- Make small May baskets from paper cups, attaching handles made of yarn or pipe cleaners. Let the kids deliver them to neighbors.

Paper Plates

- Make an embroidery kit by drawing a simple design on a paper plate. Punch holes and let the child sew with yarn or embroidery thread along the lines, using a blunt needle. Put supplies in a self-closing bag to complete the kit.

- Use paper plates as flash cards for learning shapes, letters and numbers with children. Correct answers can then be tossed like a Frisbee to celebrate the correct answer! This may help to keep the active child more interested in this learning game by letting him or her *throw* the paper plate instead of just holding onto a card.

Paper Towels

- Use paper towels as place mats when serving food to little ones. If there are spills, just wipe them up and replace the paper towel.

- Remove crayon marks from a chalkboard by placing a paper towel over the marks and pressing with a warm, not hot, iron. As the towel absorbs the crayon wax, move it to a clean spot and continue pressing. Wash the board with a little detergent and water to remove final traces.

- Freeze folded, dampened paper towels in plastic bags for cold compresses. Use as needed on bumps, bruises and other minor or imaginary injuries.

Peanut Butter
- Rub peanut butter into gum that is stuck in your child's hair. Work in with fingers and comb gum out. Shampoo as usual.

Pennies
- Hide pennies in the sandbox. Looking for money will keep kids busy. This should be done with children who are old enough not to put things in their mouths.

- Try a penny hunt at your child's next birthday party. It is healthier than a candy hunt.

Pet Chew Toys
- New plastic pet toys, if tough and well-made, are excellent for a teething baby.

Pet Food Can Covers
- Plastic pet food can covers make good tops for covering liquid infant formula. Clean well before using.

Petroleum Jelly
- If your child has frequent nose bleeds and dry nostrils, rub a little petroleum jelly on nose to keep nasal passages moist.

- Rub a little petroleum jelly into patent leather shoes to keep them shiny.

- Apply to ears and cheeks to prevent winter frostbite.

- Put it on eyebrows and above baby's eye area to prevent shampoo from running into eyes.

- Put a bit of petroleum jelly on a tissue before wiping runny noses to "soften the blow."

Piano Bench
- An old piano bench makes an excellent lift-top desk for a child. Putting small pieces of cork on the front edge as stoppers will prevent tiny fingers from getting hurt.

Pillowcases
- Standard and king-size pillowcases often make good sheets for bassinet and travel crib mattresses.

- Slip a pillowcase over a plastic baby bathtub. The water will drain right through the fabric making a soft hammock .

- Let children personalize their pillowcases by decorating them with liquid acrylic paint. Mix paint with water in equal amounts, and apply with sponge brushes. Once dry, it is washable.

- Old pillowcases can be made into drawstring bags to carry or store toys. Let kids decorate them for a rainy day project.

• When traveling, stuff a pillowcase with your child's coat or jacket, to make an instant car pillow.

• A painting smock can be quickly made by cutting a large hole at the top of a pillowcase for the head, and two at the sides for the arms.

Pipe Cleaners
• Tie up a ponytail with a colored pipe cleaner.

• A pipe cleaner makes a good emergency shoelace. Or use one to secure a latch on some types of school lunch boxes.

Pipe Insulation
• Cover sharp edges of tables and chair legs with pipe insulation to protect your toddler. Slit the tubing lengthwise and tape it closed with electrical tape.

Pizza Cutter
• Cut up bar cookies, french toast and pancakes easily with a pizza cutter. Also good for trimming the crusts off bread and cutting spaghetti into bite-sized pieces.

Place Mats
• Line the drawers in your child's dresser with place mats that you no longer use.

Plastic Mesh Canvas

• Use plastic mesh canvas to prevent kids *(and cats!)* from digging in your potted plants.

Plastic Lids

• Use plastic lids as coasters for kids' drinks.

• Make stencils for letters, numbers and greeting card designs from plastic lids. Draw the design on the lid with a marking pen and cut out the shapes with a utility knife. Hold the stencil firmly over the object to be marked and paint or sponge over it.

• Make a simple embroidery hoop for a child. Take the plastic lid from a large, round margarine container and cut out the center, leaving the rim only. Then cut off the bottom of the container. Place the embroidery cloth over the top of the margarine tub and snap on the lid.

• Cut a small hole in the top of a plastic lid and place over your child's container of paint. Show kids how to wipe off excess paint on the edge of the lid. Less spills and drips.

Playpens

• Protect your Christmas tree from a toddler's inquisitive hands by setting the tree inside the playpen.

• Use an old playpen as a large toy chest.

Ponytail Holder

• Stretch a ball-end ponytail holder over the hinge pin on the inside of a door. This will prevent the door from closing all the way and tiny fingers from getting pinched.

Popcorn

• Popped popcorn makes good flowers, apple blossoms or snow in children's collage projects.

Popsicle Sticks

• Use a wooden Popsicle stick as a skewer when serving kids foods. Hot dogs, bananas and watermelon pierce easily. Bananas can be frozen and later enjoyed as a cool treat.

• Use as safe spreaders for finger paint or pudding paint.

• Make a temporary splint for an injured finger from a Popsicle stick.

Potato Chip Cans
- Use a potato chip can to stock and hold jars of baby food.

- Decorate a tall potato chip can with wallpaper and use it to hold five-ounce paper cups in the bathroom.

- A tall potato chip can also makes a good brush caddy for kids' paintbrushes. Store brush side up, of course.

Pressure Safety Gate
- Use a pressure gate to limit a pet's access to the baby's room.

Q-tips (cotton swabs)
- Q-tips make good mini paint brushes.

- Use also as tools for painting Easter eggs, or cleaning small areas of soiled toys.

Quarry Tile
• Have kids glue school pictures to a quarry or ceramic tile and give to grandparents as a personalized paperweight.

Quilts
• Hang a thick quilt over a sunny window during naptime.

• Baby quilts make nice wall decorations. Display on a quilt rack or hang with brightly painted clothespins.

Ribbons
• Tie ribbons around stuffed toys, and then hang them from hooks from your child's bedroom ceiling.

Rubber Bands
• If you're in a group with several moms, babies, and loose bottles, mark your baby's bottle with a colored rubber band. This may help to prevent mix-ups.

Rubber Cement
• Remove crayon marks from washable wallpaper with rubber cement. Paint on a small amount, let dry slightly, then roll off.

Safety Pins
- Pin matching dirty socks together before dropping them in the laundry to thwart the voracious *Sock Dragon* in your washing machine and dryer.

Salt
- Make playdough by mixing together ½ cup salt, 1 cup flour, 2 tbsp of vegetable oil and ½ cup water. Store in an airtight container or plastic bag. Add food coloring and try adding 1 tsp of glitter for extra fun!

- Combine ¼ tsp of salt with 4 ounces of hot water to make your own saline nose drops. After the solution cools, use one or two drops per nostril every few hours.

Salt Shaker

- Fill a shaker with equal parts of sugar and cinnamon for kids to sprinkle on toast or cereal. There'll be little mess or waste.

Sanitary Pad

- When changing is difficult, line a diaper with a sanitary pad instead of double diapering a baby for a long car, bus or plane trip.

Scissors

- Let kids help in the kitchen by cutting up salad fixings with blunt scissors.

Shampoo

- Soak children's combs and brushes in a shampoo solution for easy clean up.

Shaving Cream

- Use shaving cream as a finger paint. Children can paint on a kitchen table, vinyl tablecloth or a cookie sheet. A drop of food coloring or a sprinkle of tempera paint adds color.

- Promote artistic sculpture and bath time fun by squirting a few mounds of shaving cream into the water or on the sides of the tub.

- Use a dab of shaving cream to remove a juice moustache.

Sheets

- Spread a large sheet over the back seat when traveling by car with kids. At rest stops or at the end of the day just remove it, shake it out and your car is clean. Remember to pick up paper pieces and drop them in the trash.

- Place an old fitted sheet on the bottom side of the top bunk bed so the child on the lower bunk has something to look at. If the sheet has no pattern, decorate it with markers.

- Create a stuffed animal hammock from an old attractive sheet. Fold it into a triangle, tack one point to the corner and the other two along the adjacent walls.

- In addition to the old, reliable, last-minute ghost getup, you can also turn an old sheet into an instant octopus costume by tying the sheet loosely around the neck, with eye and mouth holes cut out, then cutting the sheet into eight "tentacle" strips from the shoulder down.

- Remove your tree "needle-lessly" by wrapping a large, old sheet around it and carrying it out sling fashion.

- Place your not-yet-mobile child on a large sheet for a clean play area along with some toys. A sheet makes cleaning spit-up easy, and toy pick-up can be finished in an instant.

Shoe Bags
• Use a shoe bag near the changing table to hold baby powder and other diapering items.

• Hang a shoe bag over the back of the front seat in your car to hold toys so they are accessible to the kids in the back.

• Hang a shoe bag in a playpen. Your child can put small toys into its pockets.

Shoe Horn
• Use as a sandbox trowel.

Shoe Rack
• A shoe rack set inside of a boot tray is a good way to dry hats and mittens and catch drips.

Shoulder Pads
• Tape old shoulder pads securely to pointed corners of furniture to keep your toddler from falling and getting hurt.

• Use a shoulder pad as a strategic diaper additive for a baby boy.

• Stuff pillows, toys, and the like with old shoulder pads.

Shower Curtains

• Use a shower curtain to protect a bedwetter's mattress.

• A shower curtain can serve as a good picnic tablecloth.

• Draw on an old shower curtain with markers. Make an entire town with roads and buildings for kids to use with small cars or racers.

• Line bibs that you sew with pieces of an old plastic shower curtain. Or make the entire bib out of a shower curtain and use bias tape for the tie strips.

Shower Curtain Hooks

• Slip shower curtain hooks over the top rail of the crib and hook baby toys and rattles on them.

• Use a shower curtain hook to loop a hand towel to the towel bar.

Shower Curtain Rod Cover (plastic)

• Cut off a 12-inch piece of a plastic shower curtain rod cover and snap it on the handle of your grocery cart to provide a cleaner teething surface for your little one.

Sink Mat (rubber)
- Place a rubber sink mat on the seat of a high chair to keep a child from sliding off.

Sled (plastic)
- Take a plastic sled to the beach to carry your belongings *(and even your toddler)* across the sand.

- Or use one to collect and move toys that are spread around the house.

Soap
- A bar of soap wrapped in fabric is a good place to keep open diaper pins. The fabric will hold in the crumbs, and the soap will lubricate the pin to make it easier to poke through the thick diaper.

- Lubricate a stubborn zipper by rubbing a bar of soap over it's teeth.

- Use the bathroom mirror for messages. A bar of soap is your "pencil". Hearts and "I-love-you" notes are fun.

Socks

• Replace worn cuffs on sleeves or jackets with cut-off ribbed sections of old socks.

• Cut off the top ribbing of a clean old sock and use it as an instant knee or elbow bandage.

• Use an old sock to cover over a child's ice skates to keep feet warmer. Cut a slit in the bottom for the blade.

• Slip a sock around a baby bottle to provide a better grip for small hands.

• Fill a small cotton sock with a soap bar or soap slivers. Tie it closed and use it for a bath time sudsy washcloth and one that won't slip away.

• Apartment-dwelling families with active youngsters can keep those who live on the floor below them happy by having the kids wear big, heavy socks over their shoes.

• Make hand puppets for your kids' puppet shows from old socks or mittens. Add yarn for hair and buttons for the face.

• Use knee socks as mittens for a small child. They'll come up to the elbow and can't be peeled off easily.

Socks (tube)

• Cut thumb holes in tube socks and pull them over mittens. This will prevent icy "pills" from building up on wool mittens and can be pulled up over jacket sleeves to keep out snow.

• To clean mesh on playpens, thoroughly dampen two socks in a mixture of bleach, detergent and water. Slip the socks on your hands and rub both sides of the mesh simultaneously. Rinse by spraying mesh well with plain water. Best to be done outside.

• Cut off the tops of tube socks and use them as knee protectors for a crawling child, or as leg warmers over pants.

• Older kids can use cut off sock pieces as sweatbands on their wrists.

Spatula

• Spread ointment or petroleum jelly on a baby's bottom with a rubber spatula. This will help keep fingers clean enough to attach the tape tabs on disposable diapers.

Spice Racks

• Hang a spice rack on the wall or inside of pantry to hold jars of baby food.

• Use an extra spice rack to organize small jars of paint.

Sponges
• Freeze dampened squares of cut-up sponges to use as small compresses.

• Cut a sponge into puzzle pieces for a child. Or buy a package of different colored sponges and cut them into shapes to use as blocks in or out of the bathtub.

• Cut a hole in a sponge big enough to hold a jar of paint or rinse water to use during craft projects.

Spray Starch
• Use spray starch as you would calamine lotion for relieving chicken pox itch or other itches.

• Try liquid starch as a glue substitute in certain paper crafts.

Sprinkling Can
• Add fun to bath time by rinsing out shampoo with a garden sprinkling can.

Squirt Guns
• Fill kid's squirt guns with glass cleaner and let them help you clean windows *(preferably outside!)*. Be certain they know not to spray at each other's eyes.

Straws
• Using a straw to sip water after giving your child a pill, may make it easier to swallow.

• To keep strings on pull toys from getting tangled in the wheels, draw the string through a plastic straw, and knot it to the toy.

• To make croquet wickets more visible on the lawn, run them through colorful straws before putting them in the ground.

• To make a magic wand, just staple a star to a plastic straw.

• Let children sip cooled soup through a straw.

Stuffed Animal
• Stand a stuffed animal at the end of the bed to "protect" your child during the night.

Styrofoam Block
• Before a party, cut holes in a piece of styrofoam to use as a stand for ice cream cones. This way, you can make up cones ahead of time and pull them out of the freezer when you need to serve the guests.

Styrofoam Food Trays

- Cut styrofoam food trays into floating bathtub toy shapes. Use caution with small children who may chew on them.

- Use the flat bottom of a clean meat tray for making stencil patterns. With a utility knife, cut out stencils for your children to use in various craft projects. Secure the tray to the material to be decorated and trace around the lines or fill in the spaces with paint.

- Make simple puzzles for a toddler by pressing cookie cutters into the centers of meat trays and cutting around the outlines with scissors.

- Let your child practice stitching on a styrofoam tray using a blunt-tipped needle threaded with yarn while you're busy sewing.

Suction Soap Bar Holder

- Place a suction soap bar holder on baby's high chair to secure a bowl or plate to the tray.

Swim Goggles

- Put goggles on children while shampooing to keep soap and water out of their eyes.

Tablecloths (vinyl)

• Use an old vinyl tablecloth as a drop cloth under a high chair or children's chairs during meals.

• Use a vinyl tablecloth to protect a child's mattress.

• A vinyl tablecloth makes a great "magic carpet" for kids, especially if it's fringed.

Tape (masking)

• Use tape to hold disposable diapers when the self-stick tab DOESN'T.

Tape (transparent)

• Occupy a small child while he or she is waiting for dinner by putting a piece of tape on wrists or fingers. This also is a good trick when you are trying to photograph your baby.

• Tape a child's bangs to his or her forehead and cut *above* the tape line. You'll have a straight guideline, and the tape will hold the cut hair. Remember, bangs do shrink up when you remove the tape, and the hair dries.

• Reinforce the corners of games and puzzles boxes with tape before they begin to fall apart.

• Use several layers of transparent tape to make fake finger-nails for children. At Halloween time, shape into long witch's nails.

• Make a quick emergency bandage by taping a piece of tissue over a wound.

• Use a reverse circle of tape for a game of "Pin the Tail on the Donkey". This is much safer than using pins.

• Strengthen crayons and chalks by wrapping midsections with tape.

• Tape a newly lost tooth to a card or sheet of paper so the Tooth Fairy can find it more easily under the pillow.

• Protect beloved children's books by carefully taping the spines, the cover edges and maybe even edges of the pages to ensure longer wear.

- Make saving treasures from a nature walk easy. Put one or more bands of tape—sticky side out—around a child's wrist. Leaves, flowers and small items can be attached for safe keeping and carrying home.

- "Laminate" important items such as bus passes, lunch tickets or ID cards with transparent tape. *(It can keep them in shape even if they go through an occasional wash cycle.)* Use the same process to protect and strengthen paper dolls.

Tea Bag
- Help control bleeding when your child loses a tooth by holding a wet tea bag on the open area. With today's flavored teas *(herbal teas, however, do not work)* it can even be a special treat.

Teething Pain Reliever (liquid)
- Minimize pain when removing splinters by first covering the affected area with liquid teething pain reliever. Then re-move the splinter.

Telephone Books
- Tape two or three old phone books together with duct tape and keep them in your car trunk for an instant booster seat.

- Let a child tear up an old phone book for fun and exercise.

• Press leaves and flowers your child may wish to save in an old phone book until completely dry.

Tennis Balls
• Turn old tennis balls into coffee table edge covers. Slice a ball half-way open and push it over a sharp corner to prevent an unsteady toddler from getting hurt.

• Place a tennis ball in a sock, knot the open end and use it as a toss-ball. *(There's more for a child to catch this way.)*

Terry Sweat Wrist Bands
• Use sweat bands to protect toddlers' knees when they are learning to walk.

• Cover metal car seat buckles with terrycloth wrist bands so they won't burn children while traveling on hot days.

Terrycloth Ponytail Holders
• Place terrycloth ponytail holders around your child's wrists to keep juices and dribbles from running down arms and staining their clothes.

Thermos Bottle
• Soak a sore finger in a wide mouth thermos bottle. It will keep the water warm, or cold, for a longer period of time than a regular cup.

Timers

• Set a timer to remind yourself when a visiting child must go home.

• Use a timer to signify the end of "time out", when disciplining a child.

• Set a timer to go off two or three minutes after the start of toothbrushing time.

Toilet Paper

• Float a square of toilet paper in the bowl so a little boy can practice his "aim" when learning to use the toilet.

Toothbrushes

• Let a teething baby gnaw on a soft, new toothbrush.

• Children can make a splatter painting by using an old tooth-brush and paint. Scrub the paint through a screen onto a piece of paper. It is an especially interesting technique when the paper is first covered with leaves, flowers or stencils.

• Use a toothbrush to remove lint from the Velcro tabs on children's sneakers.

Toothpaste

- Use a dab of toothpaste on a bottle brush to scrub out sour baby bottles.

- Use toothpaste to remove tar from the bottom of bare feet by rubbing it into the tar, then rinsing off.

- With the help of a soft wash cloth, use a little toothpaste to remove a grape juice moustache from child's upper lip.

- Avoid nail holes in painted walls. Hang a lightweight poster or piece of artwork by dabbing a bit of white toothpaste on the back of each corner and pressing it firmly to the wall. When you take it down, there's only a mark to wipe off.

- Clean white baby shoes by applying toothpaste with an old toothbrush. This also works to clean sneakers.

Toothpicks

- Use toothpicks to construct foods such as marshmallows, cheese cubes or grapes into "molecules" or silly creatures just for fun.

- Use toothpicks as eating utensils in place of silverware. It may motivate a fussy eater or just be fun for a change of pace.

Towels

• Drape a hand towel over the top of a bathroom door. It will allow for privacy but will prevent a small child from locking himself or herself in.

• Layer a bath towel or two over bed linens when your child is sick. Remove soiled or damp towels as needed. This may lighten your laundry load by saving you from washing all of the bedding each time your child feels ill.

• Protect a child against burns from a hot car seat by stretching a light-colored towel over the seat.

Travel Soap Holders

• Use a plastic travel soap holder for storing playing cards that your children might like to play with at home or in the car.

T-Shirts (adult)

• Use an adult-size t-shirt as a huge bib to cover your child completely during meals or during arts and crafts activities.

TV Stand

• Turn an unused TV table into a stand for a doll house.

Umbrella Stand
• Store long-handled toys in an umbrella stand.

Upholstery Cleaner
• Spray on a soiled stuffed animal. Let dry, then vacuum or sponge off.

Vacuum Cleaner
• Run the vacuum cleaner near the crib. The humming sound will often put a baby to sleep.

VCR Camera

• Use your VCR camera to record your school-age child and show the tape to the younger sibling who may be feeling lonely.

• Demonstrate a craft activity on tape to be done by your child and the babysitter while you are out.

• Tape a play with family members. Your library will have simple scripts available. Or act out a Mother Goose tale.

• Record your child's sport activity then have the team over to view it.

• Designate a cassette to make a video tape album to record your child each year at the same time such as birthday, starting school or holiday. It will be a wonderful "fast growth" record to enjoy in the years to come.

Vegetable Shortening

• Use vegetable shortening, like Crisco, to form a moisture barrier on baby's bottom. Helps prevent diaper rash.

Velcro

• To keep blankets from being kicked off at night, attach a piece of Velcro to the edges of the blanket and the under-side of the mattress or mattress pad.

- Attach Velcro to overall straps of the child being toilet trained. Think of it as "Dressing for Success."

- Attach a Velcro patch to each mitten and stick them together for storage.

- Create your own adjustment strap for the back of a baseball cap by covering over or replacing the plastic strips with heavy-duty Velcro strips. Keep the end of a child's belt in place with a dot-size piece of adhesive Velcro.

Vinegar
- Remove decals on a painted wall by moistening them with several coats of white vinegar. The decals will soon be loose enough to lift off.

Wading Pool
- Slide a plastic wading pool under the bed to store out-of-season clothes and toys.

- Take an inflatable wading pool on a camping trip and use it as a bathtub for small children.

- Let an inflatable wading pool serve as a playpen or crib when you're traveling with a not-yet-mobile baby.

Washcloths

- Have children hold a washcloth over their forehead and eyes when you're shampooing their hair.

- Use terry washcloths for children's napkins.

- Using a RED washcloth to clean up cuts may make the necessary first aid less frightening to your child.

Washing Machine

- Place a safely secured and attended new baby in an infant seat on top of a running washing machine. The sounds, vibration and warmth *(a dryer does the same trick)* will often help a fussy baby to fall asleep.

Washer Rings (metal)

- Use metal washers as weights to anchor helium balloons when using as party decorations. Just tie washers to the ends of string and place on table or floor.

Wastebasket

- Place an easy-to-wash plastic wastebasket at the bedside of an ill child who you think may vomit.

Waxed Paper
- Buff a shine on children's shoes with a piece of waxed paper.

- Rub waxed paper over high chair tray runners to make the tray slide easily into place.

Waxed Paper Box
- A box of waxed paper *(or any similar container)* can help hold a hand of cards for the small child. Remove or cover the sharp metal cutting edge with several layers of masking tape.

WD-40
- Spray WD-40 on decals or stickers to help remove them from washable walls.

- Use it to remove crayon marks, colored pencil or Silly Putty from most surfaces, ranging from walls to leather furniture.

- Spray WD-40 on carpet or fabric to remove gum.

- Grease spots often respond to WD-40. Spray on clothing stains and let sit before running through the washer.

- Clean your Nintendo controls with WD-40.

- Lubricate your kid's outdoor slide by wiping it down with a cloth sprayed with WD-40. Use on hinges of swings to keep them from squeaking or to loosen a stuck zipper.

Xerox Copies
- Make handprints once a year of your child's hands to watch and compare growth. Label with date and child's age.

- Make color or black and white photocopies of your kids' photographs. You will save money in photofinishing.

- Before putting a child's birth certificate in a safe-deposit box, make several photocopies. You'll be surprised at how often you will need them.

- Let your child color photocopies of pictures of family members. Send to grandparents as a double treat.

Yardsticks
- Slide a yardstick through the handles of cabinets or drawers to prevent a curious toddler from opening them.

- Nail or glue a yardstick to the wall to measure your little one's growth.

Yarn
- Save yarn from gift wrap and use to tie up a ponytail or for kid's craft projects.

- Hang ornaments from a Christmas tree with yarn rather than metal ornament hooks. It's safer with kids around.

Yogurt Cups
- Turn clean, sturdy plastic yogurt cups into disposable drinking mugs for kids.

Zero Coupon Bonds
- A good way to save for your child's college education— starting today!!

Adult Uses For No-Longer-in-Use Children's Items

Turn about is fair play! Here's a list of kid's items that may just have another life now for YOU when the kids grow out of them.

Bassinet
• Use a bassinet as a laundry basket.

Baby Booties
• Save one and tie it to your key ring as a decorative —as well as a sentimental—piece.

Baby Bottle Brush
• Clean your narrow-necked vases or pitchers with a baby bottle brush.

Baby Food Grinder

- Use the old baby food grinder for chopping nuts, grinding raisins and other dried fruits, softening butter or margarine, making egg salad, mashing bananas or potatoes, and grating soft cheese.

Baby Food Jars

- Place a votive candle in a baby food jar at the bottom of a paper bag to use as a lumineria at holiday time. A grouping makes walkways look especially festive for nighttime parties.

- Also good for holding small items at your workbench or at your sewing table.

Baby Powder

- Shake baby powder generously on a grease spot on clothing and let it sit overnight before brushing out or running through the laundry. Keep a container in the kitchen to sprinkle on grease splatters on clothing as they occur.

- Sprinkle a deck of cards lightly with baby powder and shuffle if they are sticking together.

Baby Sleep Monitor

- Put the receiver of an old baby sleep monitor next to your radio or TV and take the other part with you, so you can tune in while working outside.

Baby Wipes
- Use baby wipes to clean up a variety of adult-type stains. They have been reported to have successfully removed chocolate, grape juice, butter and coffee stains from both clothing and upholstery.

- Use to clean hands after self-service gas stops.

Cloth Diapers
- Treasure old diapers as the world's best lintless dustcloths. Use them as ironing press cloths, too.

Cotton Underwear (outgrown)
- Ditto!

Crayons
- Use appropriate shades of crayons as quick furniture scratch cover-ups.

- Repair the damage on fabric done by a splash of bleach by heating the area with an iron, coloring it with a crayon in the appropriate color, and then setting the color by placing a piece of waxed paper over the repair and ironing again.

Diaper Pail
- Let the old diaper pail serve as a laundry hamper.

Formula Cans
• Use metal formula cans for baking quick breads (nutbread, zucchini bread, Boston brown bread, etc.). Grease and flour the cans and fill up halfway before baking.

Lunch Box
• Use an old lunch box to hold grocery coupons. It goes easily from house to car to store.

• Store first aid supplies in one and keep it in your car trunk.

Mesh Playpens
• Use the old playpen as a hamper under the laundry chute, as a pet corral for new puppies or kittens, or as an almost-windproof collector for fall leaves when you're raking.

Plastic Swimming Pool
• Ditto!

Plastic Baby Bottle Liners
• Unused plastic liners from certain disposable bottles can act as 3"x5" recipe card covers.

Ponytail Holders
• Use ponytail holders to contain long electrical cords.

Safety Gate
- Transform a safety gate into a sweater dryer by laying it flat, over your bathtub or laundry tub.

Stuffed Animals
- Use a small stuffed toy as a pin cushion when your child outgrows it. *(Best not to use their favorite one!)*

- Or use one to hold an assortment of your jewelry.

Vaporizor (or humidifier)
- Give plants the greenhouse treatment during the winter by using that machine you bought to nurse the kids through the flu. Run it in the rooms you keep your plants in.

TOPIC INDEX